ON THE HIGH SEAS

SHIPS THEN AND NOW

ON THE HIGH SEAS

SHIPS THEN AND NOW

Steve Otfinoski

BENCHMARK BOOKS

MARSHALL CAVENDISH
NEW YORK

Benchmark Books
Marshall Cavendish Corporation
99 White Plains Road
Tarrytown, New York 10591-9001

Library of Congress-in-Publication Data
Otfinoski, Steven.
On the high seas : ships then and now / Steve Otfinoski.
    p.   cm. — (Here we go!)
Includes index.
Summary: Surveys different kinds of ships, from John Fitch's early
steamship to the large ocean liners, freight ships, and oil tankers of today.
ISBN 0-7614-0609-3 (lib. bdg.)
1. Ships—Juvenile literature. [1. Ships.] I. Title II. Series: Here we go!
(New York, N.Y.)
VM150.086   1997   387.2—dc21   97-6039   CIP   AC

Photo research by Matthew J. Dudley

Cover photo: *Image Bank,* Richard Ustinich

The photographs in this book are used by permission and through the
courtesy of: *The Image Bank:* Steve Dunwell, 1, 26; Color Day Productions,
2; Walter Bibiko, 6; Guido Alberto Rossi, 14; William Edwards, 16;
Gary Cralle, 17; Kay Chernush, 18; Stephan Wilkes, 19; Michael Medford,
20; Ira Block, 21; Magnus Reitz, 22; Steve Proehl, 24-25; David Brownell,
28 (left); Marcel Isy-Schwart, 28-29; Albert Normandin, 30; Thomas R.
Rampy III, 32; Toby Rankin, back cover. *Corbis-Bettmann:* 7, 8, 9, 9
(insert), 10. *UPI/Corbis-Bettmann:* 11, 13. *Photo Researchers, Inc.:*
Dick Davis, 12; Porterfield/Chickering, 14 (insert); Carl Percell, 15;
C. Monteath, 23; Joseph Nettis, 27.

Printed in the United States of America

1   3   5   6   4   2

To Mom,

who deserves a long, relaxing cruise

Ships are the rulers of the seas.
They carry people and goods
around the world.
Unlike sailboats, ships don't
need a good wind to get going.
They run on fuel.
The first ship to sail under its
own power was built by American
inventor John Fitch (above).
It ran on steam power.
Fitch's little ship was not
strong enough to cross the ocean.
It carried passengers
to and fro on the Delaware River.

Poor John Fitch couldn't get enough passengers to make
his steamship pay, and he went broke.
Robert Fulton had more success.
He built the *Clermont* (above) in 1807.
It carried people up and down New York's Hudson River.
Steamships soon grew bigger and better.
England's *Great Eastern* (right) was nearly
seven hundred feet long and could carry
four thousand passengers across the Atlantic Ocean.
It also laid the first telegraph cable across the ocean floor.
The brave seaman is the *Great Eastern's* Captain Harrison.

By the early 1900s, powerful diesel engines replaced steam engines on ocean-going ships.
Luxury ocean liners like the *Normandie* from France could cross the Atlantic in about four days.

Not all voyages on these luxury liners ended well.
The British *Titanic* was said to be "unsinkable."
But when it struck an iceberg on its maiden voyage
in 1912, it sank within hours.
Over fifteen hundred passengers went down with the ship.

Jet airplanes put many
ocean liners out of business.
The jets could travel much faster.
The *Queen Elizabeth* is making
its last voyage here.
The *Queen Elizabeth II*,
is doing well, though.
Above, a man sweeps beneath its huge
propeller. It is being refitted in dry
dock before returning to sea.

Today's luxury liners are floating cities.
They have swimming pools, restaurants, and even theaters.
They carry passengers on vacation cruises to a sunny Caribbean island or Alaska's Glacier Bay.
Where would you like to go on your dream cruise?

Cargo ships carry goods, not people.
This container ship (above) carries its cargo in neat,
tidy containers. The containers are easily
loaded and unloaded.
The red cargo ship from France seems to glow
from the bright lights of the busy port.

Tugboats may be small, but many big ships
couldn't get around without them.
Their powerful engines can pull strings of barges,
filled with cargo, along rivers.
Tugs tow departing ships from the pier. These two (right) are
pushing a cargo ship sideways. A huge, heavy ship often needs
help to change direction in a small harbor.

Oil tankers are among the biggest cargo ships.
Today's supertankers are longer than the longest
luxury liner and carry over half a million tons of oil.
A flock of curious birds watches this tanker
enter the mouth of the Columbia River.
Tankers carry oil from the Middle East to as
far away as the United States or Japan.
They are often at sea for weeks or even months.

The crew must be very careful the supertanker
does not strike rocks or land.
Such an accident might cause an oil spill.
That could mean a superbad disaster for the environment!
Supertankers are so big, many ports
are not deep enough for them to enter.
The oil is unloaded through underwater pipelines.
Sometimes, it is unloaded into smaller tankers,
as in the picture below.

Ships in colder climates have other hazards to face. This Swedish icebreaker is cutting a path through frozen waters for other ships to follow.

This Russian scientific ship breaks through
the Arctic Ocean's ice with its own sturdy bow.
It will record weather conditions and other useful
information about this remote region.

Whatever a ship's mission is, its final destination is always a welcome sight for the crew. Here, the world's largest cargo ship brings its load into San Francisco Bay.

After a long voyage, a ship may need some
repair work to make it "shipshape."
These men are giving this ship's huge hull a new coat of paint.
They have their work cut out for them!
The warship (right) has been put
in dry dock for more serious repairs.

From the tiniest tugboat to the
biggest supertanker, ships carry people
and cargo to the four corners of the earth.
High winds, storms, and ice cannot
stop them from reaching port.
They are truly the rulers of the seas.

INDEX

FIND OUT MORE

Ancona, George. *Freighters: Cargo Ships and the People Who Work Them.* New York: Thomas Crowell, 1985.

Carter, Katharine. *Ships and Seaports.* Chicago: Children's Press, 1982.

Gibbons, Gail. *Boat Book.* New York: Holiday House, 1983.

Olney, Ross R. *Ocean-Going Giants.* New York: Atheneum, 1985.

Robbins, Ken. *Boats.* New York: Scholastic, 1989.

STEVE OTFINOSKI has written more than sixty books for children. He also has a theater company called *History Alive!* that performs plays for schools about people and events from the past. Steve lives in Stratford, Connecticut, with his wife and two children.